A Great Reset of Lies

By: Matthew Gilman

ISBN 9798744138332

Introduction

    I find it fascinating that the media will still call the Great Reset a conspiracy theory even though there is a book outlining the program written by a founder of the Word Economic Forum, Klaus Schwab. The book is only a small piece of the puzzle, more of a summery as what is to come. To get the whole picture one would have to also read Agenda 21, Agenda 2030, and Agenda 2050, all published through the United Nations and available on Amazon. The Great Reset is only the starting block for the entire program, an effort to use a pandemic to change world policies towards a more socialist society under the disguise of fighting climate change and the possibility of future pandemics.

    Due to the fast pace of the policies implemented under this program many of the things I talk about in here will seem outdated even though they might be a few months old. As I write this president Joe Biden outlined a plan for the US to be carbon free, absolute zero, by 2050 with new laws being passed to set goals for 2030. Strange how it lines up with the UN programs. It makes you wonder who is really running the country.

The Great Reset is written in two parts, the Macro reset and the Micro reset. The Macro is the overall worldwide effects of Covid-19 and how it was handled, also giving clues as to how future pandemics will be handled. The Micro reset covers the previous material but under the vision of people and companies implementing new rules and policies. Here is a hint as to what it says, some businesses will never come back (service industry). The Micro portion of the book is relatively short and repeats the same information.

The reason I decided to write this book is to refute what Schwab argues in the Great Reset. He wants one government to overlook policies and laws around the world to handle future pandemics while ignoring the countries that handled it differently. He would say that states like New York and Michigan did well in handling Covid-19, who also had the worst death counts and highest infection rates, while ignoring states like Texas and Florida who removed all mandates and immediately watched their numbers drop. Schwab's arguments tend to be biased and are not based on facts but rather ideas and policies the UN put into place decades before for the sake of creating a one world government.

4-25-2021

Understanding the Great Reset

To understand the great reset, you have to look back to the predecessors that came before. In the early 1990s the United Nations gathered together and put forth a plan to fight climate change and over population. If you have read a Brave New World you can easily picture what it was they decided on. 90% of land would be deemed man free zones, no tourism, no camping, just plants and animals. Then there was the farm land that would supply the food for the cities and then came the cities were most of humanity would spend its days. This kind of life would be highly regulated, the ownership of things is frowned upon and normal relationships like marriage, which encourages procreation, no longer exist. To travel involves a bike and you don't own a bike because they belong to the community. There is more to this plan but it is the first installment of the vision for the New World Order.

There have been different installments that haven't been that forthcoming until now. The Great Reset is a book by Klaus Schwab who had it released just before the lockdowns of 2020. In it he mapped out a plan for the world to use a disaster like a pandemic to change society as we know it. He envisions a socialist society where people don't own anything, free market capitalism doesn't exist, all money is digital, people will have social credit scores, and lockdowns are a permanent feature of life to keep carbon emissions down. This plan started to be pushed after it was revealed COVID-19 was a treat to the world and videos were released discussing the new world that is being worked on. "You will own nothing and be happy." The 45-minute-long video doesn't explain anything, there are no details as to what the great reset is. The whole thing plays like an ad for a pyramid scheme that someone is trying to sell you.

Currently there are several aspects of the great reset that are being put into play. The elimination of petroleum has started. President Biden put a halt to the Keystone Pipeline and during his campaign run he did state that he would put an end to fossil fuels during his administration. The food supply is moving away from animal protein due to the belief that they cause higher carbon emission unlike protein alternatives like soy and insects. Large populations of poultry and swine have been culled in the last year from fear of disease. The lockdowns have started the destruction of small businesses in favor of large corporations that are becoming more dominant in the food supply chain. Bill Gates is now the largest owner of farm land in the world.

To help further the great reset new ideologies are being forced onto the public in an effort to make "right think" the norm and to stop the questioning of these new policies. BLM and ANTIFA brought identity politics to the news with no repercussions for violating lockdown orders and massive amounts of destruction against private businesses. We also saw discussions against the ownership of private property on liberal news outlets. Free speech is being allowed for certain political beliefs while those with opposing views are labeled hate speech or insurrection. To not follow the great reset is to be an enemy of the state. President Obama set the precedent for what happens to enemy of the state with the drone assassinations of US citizens for possibly being enemies of the state. Due process does not exist for those who are considered dangerous to the general public. In the great reset ideas are weapons and those that don't fit the agenda are terroristic. Anyone opposing this ideology is an enemy of the state and can either be reprogrammed for right think or be exterminated. In the United States the Democrats, who are now in power in the house, senate, and executive branch, have discussed the reprograming of Trump supporters because of the threat they represent to their policies.

The Great Reset is not just one thing, it's not an economic policy, or social structure, environmental overhaul of land ownership, and the start of a fascist state. It is all of these things. Play along and you might get some scraps, oppose and be destroyed. Let's keep in mind that the same people who push this agenda are also the biggest emitters of carbon on the planet but the middle to lower classes are considered the biggest culprits. We shouldn't be surprised that the same people who now say they are trying to save the world are the ones most responsible for the state that things are in. The Great Reset, rules for thee but not for me, that is the lesson to be learned here.

Agenda 21 in 2021

There is a lot to digest here. With the impeachment trial
blanketing the news it is difficult to piece together what is really
happening in the world. In the last couple of weeks, we have
seen Bill Gates become the largest owner of farmland in the
United States. Immediately after this purchase he invested in the
Canadian railroad becoming their largest shareholder. All of this
happened around the same time President Biden signed an
executive order referred to as 30 x 30. The order stated that 30%
of the land in the United States would be "rewilded" and turned
into untouched wilderness. Boris Johnson also signed a bill
stating that 30% of the UK will become a rewilded wilderness.
With the increase of capital gains taxes being implemented by
the Biden administration more small farms will be sold to major
corporations as the inheritors of the farms are unable to pay the
capital gains taxes of farms that are now worth more than they

were when the family started the farm. A huge land grab of private property through the Federal tax system.

Under the UN program Agenda 21 the majority of land will be turned into uninhabitable preserves where people are not allowed to live or visit. The next stage for land is highly regulated farmland that will supply produce to the cities where the majority of people live. Cars and trucks will be phased out and railroads will become the "clean" mode of transportation for produce and materials. It is interesting to see Bill Gates putting himself ahead of the game.

In 2020 the railroads, an industry that has been hurting financially for years now, is seeing an increase in investment. The Mexican government is now receiving money from the US to update and maintain their railroads. Part of this is the reimplementation of NAFTA, a pre-curser to Agenda 21.

As of 2-11-2021 the Biden administration wants the FDA to mandate GPS tracking for crops and cattle in the US. The majority of farmers will be unable to uphold to these standards if they are enforced. However, someone like Bill Gates would be able to create a system to keep track of large amounts of crops making it legal for him to sell across the country. If a farmer does not have the data on their crops to hand off to the buyer of their produce the sale is illegal.

A further push for the Great Reset is the subsidizing of minority farmers in the US. The Farm bailout program started by Trump was cancelled by Biden in the first days of his presidency, however as part of the new stimulus plan minority farmers will receive bail out while white farmers are left out of the deal. We have seen racist policies like this in South Africa in the last decade leading to farmer suicides or the murder of farmers by the state when they refuse to leave the farm they can no longer afford. There was also the theft of farmland from white farmers to be given to minority farmers and I believe a program like that will be seen in the near future.

Agenda 21 is alive and well in 2021 and through programs like The Great Reset and Agenda 2030 we are seeing the program pushed further ahead at lightning speed. We have already witnessed the largest handover of wealth in the world in the last year. Next step is the collection of land, people forced into cities, and the control of food. This is where things are heading.

The Great Reset: Introduction

The rest of this book is a commentary on the book Covid-19: The Great Reset written by Klaus Schwab and Thierry Malleret. Some things to consider for this book, since it has two authors, it is unknown what information was added by which author. The authors state that it was written at the beginning of the Covid-19 pandemic and was published June of 2020. However, the virus was not acknowledged to be an issue until February of 2020. Lockdowns began in the United States in late March and have continued on and off since. Maybe, during a time period where people are forced to be stuck indoors two men could have put together such a book but the policies and suggestions laid out mirror previous programs started by the United Nations and the World Economic Forum. My guess is that this has been sitting on a laptop for a while and it finally had its chance to find purpose.

The introduction.

Arguments are made for the book in the introduction, laying out the opportunity that is presently available for making the world a "better" place. There are references to the Black Death that went through Europe killing anywhere from 1/3 to half of the population. The authors point out the end of serfdom and claim that the style of social order disappeared because of the plague. It is a simple argument but they leave out several factors that also took place for the change to occur. The landowners stayed in power and while the workers had more rights, there were negotiations that took place because of the lack of workforce available. There was also the cooling period that took place causing a mini-ice age after the plague which also caused a famine, dropping the population even further. It wasn't until the discovery of the new world that you finally saw an end of the effects that the plague had on Europe. This wasn't called the

Dark Ages for nothing. The influx of new world gold, lumber, tobacco, furs, and crops created a market of abundance that paved the way for the Renaissance. Whether or not this would have happened without the plague we don't know. Recent discoveries by historians tell us that China had already discovered the new world at the beginning of the 1400s and this might have led to Columbus making the voyage across the ocean. China was in constant trade with Italy during that time.

Towards the end of the introduction there is some praise given to the Enlightenment that eventually came from the Black Death but the policies pushed forward in the Great Reset counter the ideas of the Enlightenment. The rights of the individual. The ability for democracy to rule a government instead of a monarchy. The right to personal property. Free speech and the protection of shared knowledge encompass the enlightenment. These ideas had to be shared in secret with the possible repercussions being death at the hands of the church or the government. The great reset is a new religion founded in environmental justice, social justice, and communist economic reform. While the enlightenment sounds good the rest of the book counters the ideas that countries like the United States were founded on.

Another argument made for the Great Reset includes the right for women to vote. Although, I will point out that it is not made clear which country the authors are referring to. They make the claim that women were not allowed to vote until after WWII and that it was the war effort that made it possible for this advancement in women's rights. Their place in the workforce moved them into a more acceptable place in society so they could earn the right to vote. This statement is completely false. The right to vote was granted to women in 1919 and signed into law in 1920. 25 years before the end of WWII women had been voting. The downside of women entering the work force during the war was their unwillingness to leave when the men came home. Divorce rates in the 1950s were at record highs and the average pay for men and women dropped with a doubling in the number of paid laborers now in the market. The two-income household had been established along with higher taxes and more expenses. The only upside to the US economy after the war was that we were the industrial complex for the rest of the world having destroyed the Japanese and German infrastructure during the war. If you wanted to purchase a tractor, car, or plane for your business you bought it from the US.

Like any of these books and programs put out by groups like the World Economic Forum there is mention of a New Order. They didn't say New World Order but they do point out that this would be a program that impacts the world as a whole. I found it interesting how they quoted Camus in his book The

Plague, discussing the changes to society after a plague rolled through France. However, this is used as an example of something that happened even though the book is pure fiction and isn't based on a real event or disease. The dead rats found in the street were the only real sign of what was happening in The Plague. Other than that, no other clues were given as to the illness in the book.

The introduction concludes with the idea that a pandemic gives society an opportunity to change many key factors in our economy and way of life. With the introduction of a plague on the planet governments and institutions are able to change policies so that when it is over there is a new normal that people will already be adapted to. The only thing wrong with this logic is that Covid-19 is not a pandemic of that magnitude. The survival rate is still at 99.9% for the majority of the population. It did not take long to discover inexpensive drugs and supplements that fought the virus raising the survival rate. Vitamin D is a key factor in the severity of the symptoms. Hydroxychloroquine is an early therapy that can be used if someone test positive for the virus but does not have symptoms. In Africa a program called ANTICOV is working to find inexpensive drugs that will drop the death rate even further. The program started in November of 2020 and is already showing promising signs of inexpensive drugs working better than the expensive ventilators that killed 85% of the patients put on them. The Great Reset may be waiting for a pandemic to hit in order to push its policies but Covid-19 is not the pandemic needed for such a policy change.

Macro Reset

Interdependence

This section of the book compares aspects of society to boats. Each country at one time used to be their own boat but through globalization they became cabins on the same boat. Because of this independent ideology it is difficult to grasp the big picture and countries need to react to things like Covid-19 as if we are all on the same boat instead of trying to regulate what happens in our own cabins. This section made me question the movement towards populism, a desire that is growing in countries like isolationism. After all, if these countries had isolated or regulated travel as they wanted to before the Covid-19 outbreak would they have been affected like the rest of the planet? At what point are nations allowed to no longer participate in a global market or will they be forced to play along whether they like it or not?

In keeping with the boat analogy could one of the solutions to Covid-19 be isolationism and making a country a lifeboat away from the rest of the sinking ship?

Velocity

With reference to our fast-paced society the argument is made that we already accept change and at a faster pace than before. More of the world is connected through the internet and we expect things faster and more immediate. As things become faster, we equate this with the fast pace of Covid-19 moving through the world even though it follows the same pattern as a bacterium populating a petri dish. Just like the end of the dish being filled so will the new policies of the Great Reset. A quote from Hemingway is used about being broke. At first, it's a little at a time then it's all at once. This is how the policies will be rolled out. We are already seeing this with the barrage of executive orders being signed by the Biden administration and policy changes in Canada and the UK.

Complexity

The system of our society is a complex system that used specialized professions to keep things working. Because of these specialized positions it is difficult to see how one change in mortgages will affect the jobs market or college enrollment. The argument is made that nobody saw the financial collapse of 2008 coming and this is a flat out lie. Michael Ruppert warned people about what was coming two years before the housing bubble burst. Members of wall street took out credit default swaps on the mortgage bonds before they crumbled due to rising numbers of default mortgages. I saw it coming with the insane prices of houses while nobody had received a pay raise in three years. These things are not difficult to see coming and I'm tired of people who think they know better telling everyone afterwards there was no way to know.

In late march of 2020 my boss sat us down in the work room and asked what we could see next? What was coming after the lockdown? After a minute of silence I said, "civil unrest, famines, riots, societal collapse." It wasn't what people wanted to hear and so these voices go ignored and forgotten even after things happen. The people in charge say "nobody knew" to take some responsibility off their own shoulders leaving those that spoke up left out as crazies and undesirables.

Covid-19 is not a black swan event, but the consequences will be. It is not difficult to see the repercussions of Covid-19 on our society. This has been tracked since the beginning. The rise in suicide from the constant lockdowns, the closing of businesses, depression among kids, lack of trust in government and media. So far there are no consequences regarding Covid-19 that haven't been seen. They are all driven by government policies and the results are easy to see or predict. Our government keeps printing money since tax revenue is not coming in, causing inflation and later a rise in interest rates which will make the federal government insolvent unless it prints more money to pay its bills. The balance books are too far to one side for the national debt to ever be paid back and there aren't enough resources in the world to cover the damage. None of this is a black swan that nobody could have expected, it's the obvious repercussions of poor management and credit card policies.

Economic reset

"Must the economy die so that it could be resurrected in robust good health? Yes." This is from page 38 of The Great Reset by Klaus Schwab and Thierry Malleret. This is a Quote from Simon Schama describing what was done during previous pandemics, but it is used as an argument for the reaction by Governments around the globe. There are arguments made on both sides of the fence for lockdowns or keeping economies open and I have to say that the arguments for lockdowns are poor overall.

On page 44 we read "Once people began to worry about the pandemic, they effectively started to shut down the economy, even before the government had officially asked them to do so." Anyone who was paying attention for the last year knows this didn't happen. I, personally, went out and stocked up on food and supplies not knowing what was going to happen over the coming weeks. The shelves in supermarkets were bare. People could not buy toilet paper on-line. Stores closed their doors and we thought that everyone was going to die. I knew it was better to spend the money I had on something I knew I would need in the future rather than save it for when things reopened. Since then, people have started saving money, not because of the lockdown but not knowing if they are going to lose their employment because of government policies, not the virus. At the time of the initial lockdown the average American had less than $1000 in savings and could not afford a $500 expense if it came their way. The only time Americans saved money was when the stores were closed due to lockdowns and that was only if they were the people who could work from home and keep a paycheck coming in. Even then, sales on Amazon and other on-line outlets skyrocketed to Christmas sales numbers funneling money away from small businesses and straight to major corporations. This argument on human reaction regarding the fear of the virus is false.

Regarding lockdowns. On page 45 we see a line "when you do it right, nothing happens." As we know now, nobody did it right. The states with the most sever lockdown orders had the largest spikes in cases and death. New York, Michigan, and Washington state shut down major parts of their economy but continued certain operations for the sake of tax revenue. You could not go to church, but you could go to the lock liquor store and buy a bottle of gin with a pack of smokes. You could go to Lowe's and buy lumber, but you weren't allowed to buy house paint or flooring. With our current culture the ability to do an appropriate lockdown was impossible. Most homes do not have enough food to feed the occupants for more than a week. Savings are non-existent and even if people had the money to buy food for several weeks the local grocery store is designed to have food for the public it serves for a week at a time. A proper lockdown was never feasible, the virus was never going away.

When referring to returning to normal the book quotes leading experts on the subject "It is likely to be before the first quarter of 2021 at the earliest." As of 2-7-2021 the US economy isn't close to recovering with people in the service industry still unemployed, thousands of small businesses closed permanently due to the mismanagement of the pandemic, and a failed roll out of a vaccine by the Biden administration. Under president Trump there were 200,000 more vaccines given per month than the current administration who came into a system already in process and more companies producing the vaccine than before.

The fear for the economy now is that with people saving money, American households have 33% more savings than before the pandemic and in the EU its 19% higher, they will not spend it once the economy is fully open hindering the growth back to normal. It's not the virus that caused these people to hold on to their money, its fear of paying their bills when the government decides they are not essential and can no longer work. In the US we received two checks during the entire span of the pandemic. Neither would be enough to pay the bills that piled up while someone was out of work or forced to shut down. Small business loans were only for paying employees to keep them on the payroll and prevent them from collecting unemployment. Many businesses shut down knowing that their employees would collect more while on unemployment and the loan did not help the cost of keeping the business afloat like paying the owner, rent, power, water bills, property taxes, resources, or any loans that might be outstanding. Small businesses overall had no help from the federal government. During the last month, with businesses still shut down and people still unemployed, state governments are starting to demand payments back from people originally deemed

qualifying for unemployment benefits due to Covid-19.

Whatever saving these people might have will be eaten by a

bureaucratic system that is looking to cut its losses while

mishandling a situation making it more painful for the public.

What future growth could look like

Employment

"This precipitous drop-in economics activity has caused a level of pain that is hard to capture in words, as lives are upended amid great uncertainty about the future." -Federal Reserve Chairman Jerome Powell

I don't know what Powell said before or after this statement that was quoted in The Great Reset, I do know that for every percentage point that unemployment increases 40,000 people die. This figure was true in 2009 when the economic collapse was taking place and everyone acted like it was the end of the world while the great black hope was taking office and Bush signed over the life savings of a nation to Wall Street. I'm sure that the numbers are higher these days and while knowing this the leaders of our country decided to sacrifice those who would not make it through a recession for those who would likely make it through a pandemic.

Schwab makes the argument that other countries kept their unemployment down through policies that kept people employed even if they weren't working. In Germany they saw an increase of less than 1% in unemployment while the US had over 11%. What he fails to mention is that the loans the Federal Government offered to small businesses were eaten up by large corporations they were not intended for. Plus, if it was used to pay employees during the pandemic and keep them on payroll it didn't have to be paid back. The stupid thing that was added to that program was the $600 a week to people collecting unemployment curing Covid-19. For a small business it did not make sense to keep your employees on payroll when they would make more money on unemployment. The other stipulation was that it could not be used for other expenses or it would have to be paid back. If a business wasn't sure it would re-open after a lockdown it was in everyone's best interest to close and collect unemployment.

Even the people running the "plandemic" have low hopes of an economic recovery after lockdown. "Globally, a full recovery of the labor market could take decades and, in Europe like elsewhere, the fear of mass bankruptcies followed by mass unemployment looms large." Page 54.

As of 2-14-2021 Covid-19 infections are down, the death rate is down, and in the UK the daily death count has decreased by 46% since the peak and they are on lockdowns again. The people running this program know what they are doing and it no longer has anything to do with the pandemic and I wonder if it ever did? Never let a crisis go to waste. The next chapter is even more eye opening.

What Future Growth Could Look Like

"The history of radical rethinking in the years following World War II, which included the establishment of the Bretton Woods institutions, the United Nations, the EU and the expansion of welfare states, shows the magnitude of the shifts possible." Page 57

This is the chapter where BLM mottos start to pop up like at a diversity meeting for work. The new measurement for economic stability will no longer use GDP but instead have unmeasurable standards that can be changed on a whim.

"These three areas create a multiplier effect both through their own employment potential and the long term benefits they unleash across societies in term of equality, social mobility, and inclusive growth." Page 63.

Schwab clearly has a problem with capitalism even though our global economy in its previous, pre-COVID-19, system did more to bring people out of poverty than the last century did. More people worldwide have access to the internet. In China, the internet, while it is regulated by the government, is accessible to everyone in an effort to make a household a business. In countries that embrace the internet and free market capitalism people come out of poverty at a faster rate. The socialist program that Schwab is encouraging will cause more poverty and death in the long run. Considering the movement against climate change, a program that would lead to a depopulation of society, would likely be favorable to these people as opposed to lifting people out of poverty and finding meaning in their lives.

Be leery any time you see the words Equality or Equity when listening to a politician or a corporate shill. Nothing good comes from the enforcement of these kinds of policies and it doesn't take long for those organizations to crumble down into their grave from mismanagement. Social mobility I already covered and this new system of the Great Reset will not help that. However, inclusive growth, is another buzz word considering that it is not referring to helping other people reach the top of their field, it involves holding others back so that the less qualified can take their place. In the US we have seen this over the years with Affirmative Action where race is a qualification over the experience that someone might have. Some will argue that is not how it works but considering the tax breaks and other incentives that these organizations receive for percentages of their staff being of a certain background the hiring process is not about filling the position with the most qualified but checking off a box on a list of whatever racial, sexual orientation, or gender that they need to appear "woke."

So not only should you prepare for being unemployed if you are a straight white male, it gets better.

"By 2030 you will own nothing and you will be happy."
Klaus Schwab, World Economic Forum 2020

"Planned yet adaptive, sustainable, and equitable downscaling of the economy, leading to a future where we can live better with less." Page 64

The economy is not intended to recover. Your retirement plan of a 401K is not on the agenda. Owning a house with land is not on the agenda. If you enjoy a hobby of collecting action figures, typewriters, Knick Knacks, vinyl records, etc. Forget about it. Your pursuit of happiness is not their concern. The constitution as a document for civil order in the US is in the way and expect amendments to start dropping like flies over the next decade. Your right to free speech is already gone with the social apps regulating speech and even removing people for "wrong speech." All of the scariest parts of 1984 are coming true and in full effect. The last election was rigged, even though they all are, to an extent never before seen and for the purpose of imposing these policies through executive order bypassing the legal route of congress.

On 2-14-2021 President Biden stated his intent to have new gun laws in place overriding the 2nd amendment of the constitution. He is calling for gun registration. The limiting of "large capacity" magazines. The collection of "assault rifles" or the registration of. Much of this is included in the bill HR 127 which would be an organized confiscation of firearms across the country. With annual fees too high for most people to afford and insane standards to pass in order to have a license this bill set up the country for another massive confiscation of wealth with the loss of thousands of dollars per person with nothing in return. Once they take the guns, they can take whatever they want after that. Your liberty is gone and that is what the Great Reset is all about.

The Fate of the US dollar

While reading this book I was surprised, and yet not surprised at the same time, that this was so far the shortest chapter. Schwab makes the obvious conclusion that there is a chance the US dollar will no longer be the world reserve currency. He discounts new forms of currency like Bitcoin but towards the end mentions the Chinese renminbi (RMB) as a possible replacement. I'm not sure if this is a smoke screen for what appears to already be happening with some countries suggesting copying the Chinese model of doing Social Credit Scores and moving all commerce to a digital format. For years now Russia and China have been buying up physical gold and silver, paying almost double in some situations above spot price, and building vaults in their national banks to house it in. Could there be a digital currency backed by gold and silver in the future? I guess we will have to wait and see.

Schwab closes the chapter by saying that the chance of the dollar losing its dominance is unlikely. But this also follows a paragraph talking about the printing of money and how inflation will pop up its ugly head as the US continues to create more dollars to keep programs going and tax revenue declines due to Covid-19. Regardless of the pandemic the odds of the US becoming insolvent were high from zero interest rates, poor (shitty) book keeping, lack of tax revenue, and an economy that has been bleeding money into China since the 1990's. Companies like Walmart have supported the Chinese Communist Party for decades by destroying local economies throughout the US, buying cheap products from China and shipping US dollars to China to pay for cheap labor and funding China's expanse across the globe. Those dollars were also used to buy US debt through the Federal Reserve making China a shareholder in the US government by being a partial owner of the treasury credit card.

This impacts US foreign policy in obvious ways. Recently President Biden was asked about the concentration camps in China and what US policy was on it? "They have a different culture from us," was the response from the president. When it comes to congress or the current president the policy has been obvious, let China do what they want because they own us. I long for the days when we had a leader that referred to the CCP as "motherfuckers." Things drastically changed in a matter of weeks.

Whether Schwab wants to say it or not the day of the dollar is coming to a close. It would appear that those above us on the income ladder agree as certain commodities are bought up and stored away for a rainy day. Billionaires are buying land, companies, art, precious metals, antiques, and anything else that will increase or hold its value over time. Keep in mind that physical items are easier to transport wealth than actual money.

A woman wearing a $10,000 neckless doesn't have to claim it like she would if it was a briefcase filled with cash. Those who can afford it are buying Bitcoin, driving the price to $50,000 per coin, last I checked. The desire to move and own land caused a housing boom during Covid-19 that is finally coming to a close. The lack of employment and no support from the government to the middle or lower class kept people in dire straits looking at eviction in the coming months along with massive amounts of debt from the pandemic, all of this due to government policies, not the pandemic.

The mismanagement of the US dollar is not due to the pandemic as Schwab would like to suggest but the poor policies that have been in place since the year 2000. If any event was to blame for the downfall of the dollar it would be 9-11 not Covid-19. If anything, Covid-19 is the final nail in the coffin not the cause of its decline.

Societal Reset

Inequalities

Here is where we get into the nitty gritty on Covid-19 and identity politics. The same people that say we must trust the science will throw in their agendas and philosophy trying really hard to weave it into the actual science of Covid-19, and of course they fail miserably. The program at the moment tells these people to keep repeating the same thing and that maybe if they drill it into the heads of the public, they will start believing it. The following are a few examples of woke agenda rhetoric that continues to come up and actually hurts the people they claim to be helping. If they followed the science, we would already be out of this mess.

"The pandemic is in reality a 'great unequalizer' that has compounded disparities in income, wealth, and opportunity."
Page 79

At no point did Covid-19 tell itself to stay out of wealthy neighborhoods, check the back accounts of the people it was looking to infect, or target people that were just out of luck in society. Covid-19, a virus, could be the least racist living organism on the planet and the best equal opportunity asshole you could come across. Not only did it jump from bats to something else, it decided that humans were fair game as well. With the focus of fighting Covid-19 being concentrated on these social factors instead of biological factors many breakthroughs in treatment and prevention have been overlooked.

"In the US, Covid-19 has taken a disproportionate toll on African Americans, low-income people and vulnerable populations, such as the homeless."

No matter how many times they try to repeat this statement it overlooks one key factor that came to light in the early days of Covid-19, Vitamin D levels is a factor in contracting the disease or having symptoms if you do. Several hospitals did bloodwork on people who tested positive for Covid-19 to see what the common factors were and what was different. Among the difference between the people who were hospitalized and those that were sent home where higher vitamin D levels in the healthier patients. Doctors were able to drop hospitalizations in half by prescribing vitamin D to patients who tested positive but didn't show symptoms yet.

The only thing racist about Vitamin D is that the production of it takes place in the skin when you are exposed to sunlight. Plus, the darker your skin is the less you produce. If you are a black person in the United States during winter your Vitamin D levels will be low unless you are taking a supplement or working out in the sun during winter for long hours of the day. If you want to help black people fight covid-19 look at the science, not identity politics voodoo.

It wasn't until January of 2021 that Dr. Fauci admitted to taking Vitamin D as a Covid-19 preventative measure in an interview with Jennifer Garner. The next day he said officially that he recommended the cheap over the counter supplement but it has yet to appear on the CDC website along with any other preventative measures against Covid-19. To this day, (2-19-2021) gyms are closed in various states across the country, Vitamin D is not recommended to the public to prevent the worse symptoms of the disease, leaving your home in California was banned for a period of time unless you had authorization, people were arrested for being on the beach (getting sunlight), in one case a man was arrested for playing catch with his daughter in a park (then thrown into jail crammed with other people who could have been contagious with the virus, but it was for his own safety). When it comes to fighting the virus, the measures taken ensured the worse possible condition for people to be in when they contracted the disease. Being healthy gives you a better immune system, sunlight gives you vitamin D, stuffing people into crammed jails without the ability to social distance is not helping fight the disease or enforcing the law, that is being an asshole. As is common policy in the United States the healthcare industry focuses on taking care of an illness or injury after it happens as opposed to preventing it from happening. When you look at it from a financial aspect how much money would people plan to make during a pandemic if the public suddenly took vitamin D, went to the gym 3 days a week, walked on the beach on a sunny day, and played catch with their kid in the park? Infection rates would go down, deaths would decline and there would be no need for a vaccine. The rate of survival for Covid-19 is over 99%. In Japan, more people committed suicide due to the quarantine in December of 2020 than died from the virus. What is the real threat here?

Social Unrest

"If the crisis goes on for long, unemployment could hit 20-30 per cent while economies could contract by 20-30 per cent ... there will be no recovery. There will be social unrest. There will be violence. There will be socio-economic consequences: dramatic unemployment. Citizens will suffer dramatically: some will die, others will feel awful." Jacob Wallenberg, Swedish industrialist, March 2020. Pages 85-86.

This opening statement appears to be pretty obvious considering there are riots happening in the Netherlands in opposition to lockdowns. More protest sprung up with businesses opening their doors defying orders to stay closed. Mask mandates go unenforced in some areas while the federal government pushes for double mask wearing. As I write this (2-19-2021), the US unemployment rate is at 6.3%, far from the 20-30% projected. However, as policies in the United States change and with the not too distance future bringing automation into the scene, we may see a rise of unemployment after the pandemic is over. The violence we are seeing today is not from unemployment it's from the lack of liberty and freedom that the public expects and demands from the government. When security goes too far for too long you will see a backlash against those who claim to be protecting the public. At what point does the government resemble an abusive husband more than a police officer patrolling the streets?

"Over the past six years, nearly 100 African Americans have died in police custody, but it took the killing of George Floyd to trigger a national uprising." Page 86.

This statement overall, is false. The 100 African Americans mentioned were not in police custody. Most of them were armed while confronting police. In the cases of those who were not armed the police were investigated, brought up on charges and sent to prison if found guilty of wrongdoing. As for the case of George Floyd several factors are left out in this chapter regarding the large amounts of methamphetamine, cocaine, and Fentanyl in his system. Then there was the portion of the video that was removed for 6 months showing Floyd demanding that officers hold him on the ground. The knee on the neck was a properly performed technique according to the standards of the police department that trained them to do it. As for BLM being a movement caused by a pandemic, that fails to be seen. BLM is an organization run by black women for the removal of men from society. Their platform on their website states they want to dissolve the nuclear family. The only purpose George Floyd served was as an excuse to push their communist agenda into American society under the disguise of equity and equality. Add the fact that it was an election year and that we haven't heard a peep from BLM since Biden became president and I think the "uprising" argument remains dead in the water. The last time we heard from BLM was their disappointment that they were not invited to talks with the Biden/Harris administration after their alleged election victory. Never underestimate the power and stupidity of useful idiots. The only way that Covid-19 became a factor during the riots as the socially acceptable ability for a person to wear a face mask in public and not be identified while committing a crime. The riots, till this day, remain the most eye-opening aspect of these lockdowns. A man throwing a ball with his daughter in a park will be arrested for not adhering to lockdown orders. Wear a mask, go out at night, break windows, burn down a few buildings, scream "black lives matter" and you will be released in the morning by the district attorney with no charges filed. If the riots showed us anything, it wasn't about racial inequality, it was that the lockdowns didn't matter.

"Social unrest negatively affects both economic and social welfare, but it is essential to emphasize that we are not powerless in the face of potential social unrest, for the simple reason that governments and to a lesser extent companies and other organizations can prepare to mitigate the risk by enacting the right policies. The greatest underlying cause of social unrest is inequality. The policy tools to fight unacceptable levels of inequality do exist and they often lie in the hands of governments." Page 88-89.

If you want to fight inequality do not give the power to the government. If you want to look at the history of social unrest you don't have to look any further than the drug war waged by the federal government since the 1970s, the crack epidemic of the 1980s, The Violent Crime Control and Law Enforcement Act of 1994, or the wall street bail out of 2009. We could go back further, maybe look at the LA riots of 1992. None of these were caused by inequality. The problems didn't spring up due to unfair hiring practices, or bad schools. Should we really be looking to the same government that pumped crack cocaine into the streets, jailed black men at an alarming rate, left the public to rot while handing over hundreds of billions of dollars to Wall Street, that is the government that Schwab wants to fix the problem of inequality? The same government that is unable to hand out a check to the public without billions going to dead people, foreign citizens, and fraud. The government is unable to balance a check book, why would we trust them with setting things right in the world? According to the current administration the concentration camps in China are okay because they have a different culture from us. I do believe that the German's had a different culture from the US before WWII but maybe our standards have changed since then. The only thing the government has proven themselves good at its mismanagement of funds and making bad decisions. If Schwab thinks inequality is bad now, wait until the government steps in to fix it, he hasn't seen anything yet.

The return of "big" government

"It matters enormously whether your country has a good health service, competent bureaucrats and sound finances. Good government is the difference between living and dying." Page 89.

If this statement is true then we have to admit that most of the world, especially the US is fucked. We already have big government. When congress passes the Equality Act, mandates the limitation of words in public speaking, and ruins the lives of people for having different beliefs as them, at what point does government go from small to "big." Our bureaucrats are incompetent in the ability to send out a check to the people who should get them. Unemployment is cut off to those who need it and paid into the system for decades until they needed it. Laws are created out of thin air and not questioned by law makers even when they don't make sense and do not hold up to science. Rioters and looters walk free while gym owners are sent to jail for keeping people healthy during a pandemic. As for finances...

Our current national debt is over 28 trillion dollars and congress wants to add another 1.9 trillion during a year where tax revenue will be down and there isn't a sign that the economy will get better in the near future. A wise man once said, "government has killed more people than a virus." If I had to choose between making my own choices to live a happy and healthy life during a pandemic or letting the government do it for me, I would choose my own judgement over a bunch of office trolls any day. The government's inability to manage healthcare for decades now isn't going to drastically change overnight. Firing the deep state and replacing our elected officials with competent people isn't going to happen. As for finances, if the government was run as well as the officials own bank accounts, we would be the wealthiest country in the world, however these old crow foot wearing, leather skinned, bags of bloated pig fat are too busy stealing from the rest of us to run the damn country in a positive way. Covid-19 will not solve this and Schwab needs to share whatever he was smoking with the rest of the world to think that it is even a possibility.

"A few examples illustrating the point strongly suggest that this time, as in the past, taxation will increase. As in the past, the social rationale and political justification underlying the increases will be based upon the narrative of "countries at war." Page 90.

America is broke. We hold several IOUs and at any point one of the countries we owe will call on our debt and we will have nothing to offer. If the government tries to say we are at war the justification will not hold and people will resist. To say we are at war with a virus that has a 99.9% survival rate is

ridiculous. It's like saying Canada is a threat and we need to start

fighting back for their poor choice in music exported to the

states. 99.9% of people who listen to Canadian pop stars don't

usually kill themselves, but listen to Nickelback or Alanis

Morissette too many times and you might want to put a bullet in

your head. Does this mean we should go to war, tax the public,

and make everyone's life a living hell to save the .1% of people

who make poor choices? No thanks, plus we know that the

money they take from us will not go towards the efforts they say

they are. It will go to black farmers because the bank account of a

poor black farmer is different from the bank account of a poor

white farmer. Or maybe they money goes toward critical race

theory therapy programs. Or gender studies in a country like

Pakistan where most of the population is Muslim and gender is

pretty well defined by their religion. The point is that the government can come up with all kinds of excuses to tax the hell out of people, a war on Covid-19 won't fly and I doubt most people would pay a drastic increase when they don't have to.

"They should also ensure that partnerships with business involves government funds are driven by public interest, not profit." Page 92.

When government offers to pay a certain amount of money for a product it is in the company's best interest to make the product for the lowest possible price to profit the most they can from the deal. We have all heard the stories about the army paying $50 for a hammer and $120 for a toilet seat. After working for a few non-profit companies, I can tell you for a fact they are not interested in saving money. These places are designed to share the wealth as long as the money travels to the top of the food chain. If Pfizer had the public interest at heart, would they have rolled out a vaccine, skipping several safety steps and studies, and shipped out millions of doses without knowing

what the possible side effects were of a never-before-seen mRNA

vaccine?

"Central banks decided to cut rates and committed to

provide all the liquidity that was needed, while governments

started to expand social-welfare benefits, make direct cash

transfers, cover wages, and suspend loan and mortgage

payments, among other responses. Only governments had the

power, capability and the reach to make such decisions, without

which economic calamity and a complete social meltdown would

have prevailed." Page 92-93.

This statement tries combine several different policies

together as if all governments implemented these policies and

ignores the countries that didn't lockdown or take drastic

measures. Central banks have left rates low since 2001 and they

haven't gone up since then. Social-welfare benefits are one of the main reasons that the economy is struggling to get back on its feet. When a person is making more money on unemployment why would they want to return to work? The direct cash transfers are a joke and an insult. If $1200 is going to change your life, Covid-19 is not your problem, you are your own problem and you need some fixing before worrying about a virus. Several countries delt with loans and mortgage payments in a different way. In the US some states suspended rent payments and mortgage payment but with the understanding that the amount owed would be paid at the end of the set time period. If people haven't been working, how are they going to pay three to six months' worth of rent at one time. Most households had less than $500 in savings before the pandemic. In Italy, the government stepped in and said that during lockdown people didn't need to pay rent, the landlords did not need to pay their mortgage, and banks and loan companies were not to take payments.

Everything was frozen in the economic system and when it was over, they would all continue as if the lockdown never happened. I found this to be the best policy and I was disappointed that others didn't follow its example. As for the argument that these policies prevented calamity and social meltdown, no it didn't. Now we have anti lockdown riots happening. Camps are being proposed in several countries to lock people up in if they are suspected of having the virus. The governments are creating the meltdown and they continue to push people further towards destruction.

"...To preventing banks from incentivizing consumer debt." Page 94.

Are we serious here? What world is Schwab living in? While we look at the crappy system, we currently live in that pushes people into debt what about the companies that work through a debt system, or the governments, state to federal, who work with a massive amount of debt. Our whole economy, because of interest rates, is based on debt. As long as there are central banks there will be debt. The banking system itself relies on loaning money that could never be returned to keep people as indentured servants for the majority of their lives.

This was a difficult chapter to read considering the amount of misinformation and half-truths thrown in to make it sound like Covid-19 was a good excuse to create "bigger" government than what we currently have. During my lifetime I have seen nothing but expansion of the Federal government. There was the Patriot Act, the creation of the Department of Homeland Security, the merger of Big Tech and the Federal Government. I don't know how much bigger Schwab thinks governments need to become in order to create his new world order but he better keep in mind to stay off my lawn.

The Social Contract

"For decades, it has slowly and almost imperceptibly evolved in a direction that forced individuals to assume greater responsibility for their individual lives and economic outcomes. Leading large parts of the population (most evidently in the low-income brackets) to conclude that the social contract was at best being eroded, if not in some case breaking down entirely." Page 96.

I don't know what social contract Klaus Schwab, a man who has worked for a university since the early 1970s and hangs out with billionaires and politicians in his spare time, was a part of or what he thought it entailed but yes personal responsibility is an idea that is important for society and mental wellbeing. The notion that personal responsibility is a bad thing might be the reason that the left has gone after Dr. Jordan Peterson time and time again. For a program like the Great Reset to work would mean that the public believes they are not responsible for their own wellbeing. In order for the great reset to happen all personal responsibility needs to be handed over to "big" government who knows what is best for you, instead of you. When this has happened in the past millions of people died. Mao knew what was best when he had the country growing only rice, causing a famine that China had never seen before. When the Tibetans were forced to grow crops they had never seen before, they starved unable to grow the new crop in a cold, high altitude environment. Stalin took farms away from people in the Ukraine and handed them over to people who had never farmed before. Millions staved and the soviet government had to produce posters telling people not to eat their children during the winter months. Needless to say, I would rather deal with a social contract where I can blame myself for what is happening in my world then point the finger at a government that never takes responsibility for the horrible things it has done.

"Today, the fundamental reasons underpinning the loss of faith in our social contracts coalesce around issues of inequality, the ineffectiveness of most redistribution policies, a sense of exclusion and marginalization, and a general sentiment of unfairness." Page 96-97.

Inequality hasn't been in issue until a bunch of communist, feminist, lesbian, trans rights activists started marching in the streets, setting fires to small businesses, and killing people in the name of Black Lives Matter. Equality is a buzz word, something to get people motivated behind. It sounds good therefore it must be, but when we look how equality and equity are used by these organizations, including the World Economic Forum, we see that the definition changes to fit their narrative and keep the conversation moving towards their end goal. If people took personal responsibility for their actions, then conversations revolving around inequality wouldn't happen. This argument assumes that people in general are not in control of their own lives and need someone else to aid them through life.

As for redistribution policies, most people do not like the idea of having their money handed over to an organization that takes a cut for themselves then hands the rest over in the most inefficient way possible. The theft from those who are responsible to hand over their earnings to those unable or unwilling to better their own lives is never look upon as a good thing. As of February 2021, a group of investors took their money and bought stock in GameStop, a brick-and-mortar video game store that looked like it was going to go out of business. In doing so, a group of hedge funds started to look at massive losses having shorted the stock trying to make easy money and kill the company all together. These people took personal responsibility for their finances and turned the game of the stock market on its head. Again, the people who took personal responsibility for their situation and bettered their lives were portrayed as villains instead of the American entrepreneurs they are. There is an agenda to teach the public to put their trust in the government and not to try solving their problems on their own. We have seen this time and time again. When wall street looks at the public, they say that they could do what they do but choose not to. When they do participate in the stock market the same people who pushed the idea of getting themselves out of poverty then scream "NO! Not like that!"

"Whichever form it takes, in almost all cases, the establishment's response has been left wanting- ill prepared for the rebellion and out of ideas and policy levers to address the problem." Page 97.

This passage was in regard to the rise in populism in many western countries like the UK, France, and the US. In the side margins I wrote as a note, "no shit." Even after Joe Biden took power along with the rest of the Democratic left their first priority was to impeach the former president of the United States. The $2000 checks that were promised to the public for voting them into office were reduced to $1400, for some people, if you qualify. As of March 2, 2021, these checks have still not been approved by the senate and will like not ship out to those in need until April. The left's lack of focus on anything other than "Orange Man Bad" continues to become more obvious and I can't wait to sit back and watch them eat each other. As for the "rebellion," the notion that the opposing side of a political view is now regarded as a rebellion or insurrection only divides the country more and serves no purpose other than to villainize people and reduce them too less than human. With Trump out of the picture the left is out of ideas, pulling a check book out to cover cost for things they cannot afford, playing the same game of kicking the can down the street to leave for someone else to clean up.

"How can it be that a person who has spent more than ten years training to become a medical doctor and whose end of year "results" are measured in lives receives compensation that is meagre compared to that of a trader or a hedge fund manager?" page 98.

I hate it when I see arguments like this. We could make so many comparisons asking why this person is poor doing this job while that person is rich doing nothing. For thousands of years people have asked these questions. The Buddha answered "life is suffering." The notion that doctors are poor is mis-leading as well. I recall a conversation, while working in an ER, and the staff was discussing "Obamacare." One of the doctors was upset that the government was going to be stepping in and regulating what he would be making. This never happened but it was being discussed at the time. His argument was "why should the government step in and change my life plan thirty years into my life. If I plan to have four houses, three cars and two ex-wives I should be able to have that." This does not sound like the complaint of a poor man who wishes the government would step in and change his pay to be comparable to a hedge fund manager. The argument continues with the Great Reset crowd, asking why the medical community is paid so bad? Depending on the level of schooling a nurse can make $40-50 dollars and hour. If they specialize in a certain field like being anesthesiologist assistant there is a good chance, they are making more money then the doctor doing the surgery because of the insurance and other cost of the profession. These are things that are considered when these people choose these fields. The amount of pay that you can earn in healthcare is equivalent to the level of education you have. The only exception is in administration. At the hospital I worked at the director made $3.3 million a year and he had never passed meds, wiped a butt, started an IV, performed surgery, or did chest compressions. By the time he was done running the hospital it was in debt and he received a massive payoff for retirement. His previous experience was running United Way.

The average hedge fund manager is a college graduate who specialized in math or a stem field and decided on investing because the money was better. The same is true with hedge fund manager Dr. Michael Burry, best known for the film The Big Short. Burry is a physician who realized he was better at investing than he was being a physician. When you look at the amount of work it takes to run an office why wouldn't someone choose to look at numbers all day instead? Burry warned people about the housing bubble in 2008. He is warning people about the inflated level of the stock market now. As for hedge fund managers making too much money, the playing field may have changed. Take a large group of people talking on Reddit, have them invest a few hundred dollars into a stock like GameStop and watch as the money pours out of the pockets of hedge fund managers as their shorts turn into a major liability.

Schwab argues that these fields need to be regulated. He makes the childish assessment that life is not fair and somehow government, and his ideas, can somehow fix this. We are already seeing this play out with the Biden administration's policies with the Covid-19 relief bill. In the bill it sets aside money for black farmers hurt financially during the pandemic while not aiding white farmers because of the color of their skin. In someone's mind this is "fair." Ask the farmers what is fair and you will likely get another answer. Be leery of anyone in power who thinks they are going to set the world right. Usually there is a trail of bodies behind them.

"Young people have a deep desire for radical change because we see the broken path ahead." Page 102.

This quote is from the New York Times article where a college junior is being interviewed. My guess is that this junior skipped his history class during his sophomore year. Young people don't have a deep desire for radical change, destroying what is before you is easier than working hard to make things better. ANTIFA and BLM march in the streets and set buildings on fire because it's easier than putting a black child through college. The actions of their "protest" (riots) did little to help black people in the country if anything it divided the country more in a way it did not need to go. The path that college students see isn't broken it just looks hard. The long hours and determination to create something without knowing if it will work is a scary thing to see. The easiest way to avoid a disappointing life is to not try at all therefore you can't ever say you failed. But you can also never say you accomplished anything either. I knew several of these people twenty years ago, friends now long gone having given up on their dreams. This idea has been pushed on our current generation through television and film. The 2009 movie, Mr. Nobody tells the fictional story of a man that nobody knows. His life has different paths and tales told in a way that tells the audience that it doesn't matter what you choose in life it all turns out the same. The message some of my former co-workers took from the film, "don't bother trying because it doesn't matter." This is what art and culture are giving us these days. We now have a do-nothing generation that expects everything on a silver platter for the privilege of accomplishing nothing. Schwab points out how unfair life is then offers the world to an unmotivated generation on the backs of the same people he says are being paid unfairly.

Who is going to pay for this radical change? The doctors and

labor force that pay for everything already. You want to know

what's not fair? Forcing people to pay for those who choose to do

nothing.

Globalization and Nationalism

"The shortening or relocalization of supply chains will be encouraged." Page 108.

In the past year there have been two events that really showed how fragile our supply chain is, Texas and Covid-19. Throw in the blockage of the Suez Canal and you get the full picture. During the Ice storm that hit Texas in February of 2021 supply chains shut down from the farm to the supermarket when the power was shut off in certain parts of the state. Ranchers could not open the doors to some of their barns to feed their cattle. Crop farmers could not work the grain silos to move feed for the ranchers who needed it. Warehouses did not function and stores were shut down unable to process purchases without electricity. Texas was a prime example of how our supply chain can be shut down with the flip of a switch.

Towards the beginning of Covid-19 the public learned how much of our pharmaceutical industry is now located overseas. India and China supply the US with the majority of our generic drugs and antibiotics. When the lockdowns started both of these countries refused to export any medical equipment or medications regardless of who owned the company or already paid for the product. Our healthcare supply chain was shut down by foreign countries.

Localizing supply chains is not a new concept. For the past twenty years I have heard people pushing this idea and to a greater extent I want to agree with it. But, if we are shortening supply chains, taking more hands away from the product to move it from the origin to your home, why is it costing more than something imported from China or India? I may like my farmer neighbor Bob down the street but I'm not going to pay double for his spinach compared to what the local supermarket brought in with Chile on the label. If localizing the supply chain is going to work the local producers need to start offering prices that will under bid what is coming in from the world market.

"On the left, activists and green parties that were already stigmatizing air travel and asking for a rollback against globalization will be emboldened by the positive effect the pandemic had on our environment (far fewer carbon emissions, much less air and water pollution.) Page 108.

Green parties will be pushing for more climate change restrictions on economies all over the world, however Covid-19 did them no favors with what we learned after the initial lockdowns. From march 2020 to the end of the year the earth heated up by half a degree. The air was cleaner but that also meant that more solar rays were able to hit the earth's surface and not be reflected back by aerosols. Reducing carbon emissions and air pollution heats up the earth faster, not slower. We learned this twenty years ago after the days following 9-11. When airlines were shut down and people stayed home from the shock of what happened with the World Trade Center, the earth, just like during the lockdowns, heated up from the lack of air pollution. As the decades pass, we continue to relearn the same things while continuing to pass along the wrong information to future generations. I remember learning about global warming as a kid growing up in the 80s and the information that is given to kids today is almost identical regardless of everything we have learned. The earth is changing, it always has been. With the agenda to shut down carbon emissions and fossil fuels we have to learn time and time again that doing so would speed up the disaster waiting to happen with harsher consequences.

"There cannot be a lasting recovery without a global strategic framework of governance." Page 113.

"Put bluntly, we live in a world in which nobody is really in charge." Page 114.

If this book is supposed to make an argument for a one world government, then they are not doing a good job. When I look at the failures of the last year, the tens of thousands of dead at the hands of people who are praised for doing the "right thing," and how other states and countries breezed through the pandemic by not changing anything in their society I have to wonder why we would encourage a system where one idiot thinks they know best and how many people would die from their mistakes? It is because of the lack of unified rule that I have some confidence that we will move past this depressing period of time. As I write this, Texas is completely open with no restrictions on its population. Mississippi no longer requires mask. Florida is opening up along with California. The list of states continues to grow and the Federal government couldn't be more pissed off about it. The moment that Texas announced they were done with lockdowns the flood gates opened for everyone else to follow suite.

The phrase "nobody is really in charge" is inaccurate to say the least.

"This failure is not the WHO's fault. The UN agency is merely the symptom, not the cause, of global governance failure." Page 118.

The WHO is a failure and continues to be a failure, unable to function outside of the prying eyes of the CCP (Chinese Communist Party), the results that we have seen are pathetic at best. The WHO was not allowed in China until the start of 2021, more than 9 months after the initial outbreak in Wuhan. Even when they did go to Wuhan the WHO did not go to the infectious disease lab that many experts speculate the virus came from. When the WHO left Wuhan, they said that their data was inconclusive and that they could not say China was the source of the virus. This whole process is absurd, try to figure out what happened at a crime scene 9 months after it happened and billions of people have moved through the area destroying any and all evidence.

To say that nobody is in charge ignores the obvious group running the world right now behind the scene, China. The main financial support for the WHO is China. The official story behind Covid-19 was written by China and handed over to the WHO. Any failures in global governance that Klaus Schwab has an issue with he can take up with China. China refused to reveal that the virus was contagious when they knew that it was. China refused to let the WHO into Wuhan when the outbreak started. China said that the virus was not spread person to person and the WHO repeated it as if it was a fact. It wasn't until the virus had passed borders into Europe and North America that the

WHO finally said we were in a pandemic. We had to wait for the obvious to happen before people would react.

A group of men wearing mask park a car outside your bank. They step out carrying guns in their hands. The teller asks you, the manager if she should call the cops. "No, its fine it's not a robbery." The men shoot the guard outside. "And now?" she asks. "they aren't robbing the back." The doors open and one of the men shoots the ceiling. "And now?" You look around realize that the robbery is happening but now it's too late. The world watched as the virus spread but the picture was always developed two weeks after it was taken. Symptoms start to show after 14 days of contracting the virus. Once you have your first confirmed case the virus has been spreading for two weeks and nobody knew. In a global economy and a global system waiting for confirmed cases was the dumbest policy and only ensured that the virus would spread and kill enabling inhumane policies like the great reset. The failure of dealing with the pandemic starts at the top including the UN, the World Economic Forum, the EU, and the WHO. Had it not been for the political situation in the US things might have been different except when the borders were closed a certain party on the left called the president at the time a "xenophobe" and a "racist." The stopping of a virus that could have had a high mortality rate was not a priority for some people until it worked for their advantage. Every country has their political problems, their social problems, and their economic problems. A global government is not going to magically solve these problems and work for every culture on the planet. To try to implement a system of one rule government will cause a backlash of violence. To really look at what Schwab is suggesting I have to ask if this is any different from the Spanish coming to the new world or the British pushing their rule over other lands like India for example. Why is the idea of the Great Reset something that everyone should or needs to follow?

The US needs to be a lifeboat for the rest of the world. The current administration is set on following the Great Reset regardless of how the public, who "elected" them, thinks about it. On a positive note, we have a constitution and the idea of state's rights. For Texas and others to no longer follow the CDC or the WHO for Covid-19 protocol is a positive sign for where this program might end up, in the trash. The more states refuse to follow the guidelines of the federal government the more the public can see which policies work and which ones don't. When given the option of having less freedom after a year of lockdowns or being open and returning to normal the answer is obvious. That is what the Biden administration fears the most, losing control of a public who were following pandemic guidelines. If people no longer fear the virus, how will they follow guidelines to solve climate change or systemic racism? There is a long list of non-existent problems that the left wants you to worry about, but when they create the problem, and only they have the answer to the problem, it's like any other religion. You enter wanting answers to something, you are given a certain truth and then spend your time trying to spread the word and fighting to make the world a better place in that image only to learn later that you are the new asshole of the world making things worse for people, not better. Nobody likes a new convert to a religion and the religion of social justice has many new coverts that are pissing people off across the globe. There is hope. More people are saying "no." The word is getting out about these clowns and their weird ideology. The people who scream about racism are finally being called out as the racist they admit to being. The damage is done and while BLM was marching through the streets setting fires to businesses and killing people the supporters in officer had Covid-19 positive patients put into nursing homes killing the elderly by the tens of thousands. Nobody marched in the streets about these policies. The last thing that the US needs to do right now is take orders from a one world government of people who are not elected and obviously know less than the people who should be running things. We can't keep track of the criminals that are currently running the country, why would we trust the criminals running a world government?

Impact of the pandemic on climate change and other environmental policies

It didn't take long for some people to figure out that this was the real agenda behind the lockdowns and policies being put into place during the pandemic. News stories continue to roll out talking about the clean air and water that happened during the lockdown. Some of these articles even call for lockdowns to help with climate change because of the effects we have already seen on the planet. There are two very important pieces of information that these reporters leave out. The earth grew hotter by .5 degrees in 2020, the largest spike in temperature for a single year. We also know the same thing happened the days following 9-11-2001 with airliners being grounded for a week. With cleaner air comes a warmer planet. I'm not saying we should pollute more, but it would appear that the only thing holding back rapid global warming is the same pollution that is causing much of it.

At this point human existence is a double-edged sword. If we try to clean up our act with carbon emissions and air pollution, we speed up the warming of the planet. If we continue on as normal, we face a slow terminal disease that will eventually kill us.

There is a man named Guy McPherson who started to speak about human extinction in 2010. Oddly enough his prediction for a terminal planet appears to fit the time line that Klaus Schwab and the UN are following with the Great Reset and Agenda 2030. Guy doesn't see humanity making it past the year 2030 because of climate change and the eventual loss of environment needed for human life. I don't know if the UN or the world economic forum are listening to Guy, but it would appear that they received the same information at some point. Could the Great Reset be a last-ditch effort to save mankind? If so, why would the creators be so selfish as to add in their own social agenda of identity politics and communist policies?

As I write this Biden, Macron, Trudeau, and Boris Johnson have signed bills making 30% of the land in their country's untouchable wild lands. This policy is in agreement with the UN's Agenda 21, started in 1992. Along with the preservation of land comes the phasing out of gasoline automobiles. The UK already set a deadline for the year 2030, which most experts admit is an impossible task. The Biden administration is also set to make a plan for 2030 regarding automobiles. Fracking was already halted on Federal land and already gasoline is 75 cents higher than it was last year. In two months, the US went from the number one producer of oil to number 5. While we were energy independent, we are set to import more oil than we export in 2021, and the countries we are buying from have people in the streets screaming "death to America." Meanwhile, with Biden as president gasoline will continue to rise as Russia and Saudi Arabia continue to keep their production down to raise the price of oil per barrel putting pain on the US consumer who has to fill their gas tank to go to work. The current administration will not care about this considering that gasoline cars will not exist by policy in 2030. The cost of this change will be passed onto the consumer who will not be able to afford it. What is not being taken into account with these new policies eliminating combustion engines is the amount of oil that goes into the production of a car regardless of what it runs on. There are seven gallons of oil per tire on a car. The plastics used throughout the car including most of the body. Shipping parts to various facilities in the assembly process. Transporting the cars to dealerships. The transportation of materials for the productions of the car. The list goes on and on for how much oil goes into the production of an automobile. We can't pretend that they don't know this. They don't want us to own cars anymore. The experiment of the automobile, or horseless carriage, is coming to a close and it's not an extinction of its own choosing. There are 800 million cars on the roads of the world and we cannot change the fuel source or motors of these vehicles to run on anything else.

Two years ago, AOC introduced the green new deal, a plan to completely eliminate carbon emissions in the US. This plan was dramatic and would cost $93 trillion dollars if it was implemented. It would also eliminate the airline industry, which means that any place relying on tourism would be dead. Nobody would be allowed to go anywhere. International trade would die. In the end the planet would die as well because of the loss of aerosols in the air reflecting light back and cooling the planet enough to sustain life. It would appear that the ultimate goal of the Great Reset, the green new deal, and agenda 2030 is to create a feedback loop of worse environmental conditions that they would have to fix and in doing so making matters worse. It's the usual pattern of needy people, create problem, fix problem that

creates bigger problem, repeat. The climate is not what appears

to be the problem, it's the people in charge.

Contact tracing, contact tracking and surveillance

"The most effective form of tracking or tracing is obviously the one powered by technology: it not only allows backtracking of all the contacts with whom the user of a mobile phone has been in touch. But also tracking the user's real time movements, which in turn affords the possibility to better enforce a lockdown and to warn other mobile users in the proximity of the carrier that they have been exposed to someone infected." Pages 160-161.

Let's be honest here, for years now the NSA has been doing what is described up above. The recent shooter in Boulder Colorado was on the FBI watch list and was able to buy an AR-15 and shoot ten people six days later. I know that this suddenly changed from pandemic to gun control, but hear me out. Just like the failure of stopping a mass shooting on behalf of the FBI, the CDC will not be able to stop the spread of a pandemic by following every citizen digitally. This section talks about proximity but it does not discuss the usual method that a virus is spread, droplet. The CDC starts to look into patient zero and finds that they were on a train for thirty minutes returning home from work. There were a dozen other people on the car. But let's say this person had a disease like Ebola which is spread through body fluids. Patient zero sneezes into his hand, puts his hand on a rail before leaving, and exits the train car. None of the other passengers touched that hand rail but yet according to this paragraph those are the ones who will be contacted and put into isolation even though they are not at risk. Meanwhile, several people board the train over the next hour, touching the handrail, following by their eyes, nose, mouth, biting their finger nails, etc. Now you have infected people and nobody will know until they start to show symptoms. Digital surveillance is a nightmare waiting to happen and we already saw what can happen when the wrong people are using it like in China.

The Risk of Dystopia

"As the last few pages have exposed beyond a reasonable doubt, the pandemic could open an era of active health surveillance made possible by location-detecting smartphones, facial-recognition cameras and other technologies that identify sources of infection and track the spread of a disease in quasi real time." Page 168.

To be fair this section of the book sounded like a general warning of what could happen if policies are put into place and expanded beyond what is considered safe for society. It is difficult to know if this was added as an insurance policy against what will likely happen so that the authors can say "we warned you" instead of "this is what we wanted." This chapter maps out what could happen if surveillance is taken to new extremes.

While the book focuses on the spread of diseases in the near future it is not difficult to see this same technology being used to control the population in regard to climate change, social justice, or pollution. Could we receive warnings via cell phone saying that our stop to the local grocery store was not justified because we didn't buy enough to warrant the trip and the carbon emissions created? Maybe our cellphone hears us using a word that is no longer allowed even though it was said in the privacy of your own home and now you have to pay a tax or a fine for saying it. In China we are already seeing trash cans that monitor how much food is being thrown away and penalizing these people for wasting food.

The people who implement these policies don't think they are creating a dystopia. Nobody in history ever thought they were making the world worse than it was before. Stalin thought that he had created paradise but in doing so it was against the law to criticize the new society that he had created. Mao thought that he was standing up for the little guy while invading Tibet, changing the social structure, outlawing any symbols of the "old way" and in the end millions of people died. None of these people thought they were doing more harm than good. In the future, will people look back at those implementing the Great Reset and wonder how we could have gotten things so wrong by following a policy that will, in the end, kill billions of people, for what is considered, the greater good?

There are two movements that are happening at the moment. One pushes the ability to monitor the public through cell phones that the majority of people own. The other is looking at using less or no technology in order to save the planet. The mostly peaceful anti-technology protestor Theodore Kaczynski wrote a handful of books about technological slavery and an anti tech revolution. In the last year Greta Thunberg, the now 18-

year-old environmental activist, has been writing Kaczynski trying to figure out a way to push an anti-tech agenda in order to save the planet. If people starting tossing their cell phones aside and start to live a life with less where does that leave the CDC with contact tracing and monitoring the public? I have to say that this is not such a bad idea, minus the mail bombs and killing innocent people. The FDA is in the process of requiring farmers to have GPS coordinates for all of their crops in order to sell their product, but where does that leave the Amish? There are still large populations of people who do not participate in the modern world and I am happy to see that they are there. It's a control group in a scientific sense of the word. During Covid-19 the Amish have refused to wear mask because they believe that only sinners can catch the disease. We have not seen any numbers for the infection rate of the Amish during the pandemic. These people do not own cell phones or travel very far from their homes, but they still interact with the general public through trade. Furniture stores and grocery stores remained open and yet we did not hear about anyone in the Amish community contracting Covid-19. In a place as rural and remote as Amish community how does the CDC do their job in contact tracing and isolating the disease? Or do they not care?

WTF did that just say?

While reading the Great Reset by Klaus Schwab I came across several lines that left me baffled and thinking WTF? The first example I will give involves something that has absolutely nothing to do with the pandemic or Covid-19.

"...the issue of systemic racism raised by the Black Lives Matter movement." Page 123.

In the margin I even wrote "WTF" unable to figure out what this had to do with Covid-19, the Great Reset, or the topic of the chapter, a rivalry between China and the US. There was no reason to mention BLM, systemic racism, or the riots of 2020 in this book at all. The short-minded people who keep trying to tell us that Covid-19 helped us realize that systemic racism exist are the same who apparently forgot that there were riots in 2014 at the height of the Obama administration. Maybe they could look back at the LA riots of 1992, or take a look at the 1960s and figure out that we have been here before and we handled things much better than the garbage policies that are being passed now to satisfy a mob. It is not surprising to see that even China brought up BLM and the problem of racism in the US during a meeting where we tried to bring up the concentration camps housing Uighur Muslims. I believe this was planned ahead of time in order to discredit the US as the world police.

Black Lives Matter, the communist, anti-nuclear family, anti-men, anti-American organization, didn't rise up because George Floyd was allegedly killed by police officers. They rose up because it was an election year, with the lockdowns the focus could be on them, the support of the democrats seeking power needed their help as useful idiots to get elected and they did the job they were asked to do. The first complaint that BLM had after Biden was elected, "he won't return our calls." Like a used slut, BLM was tossed aside once the job was done never to be called again unless a booty call of riots and arson is needed in the future.

The notion that Klaus Schwab thinks that systemic racism is real only helps my argument that this is more made-up shit that is about control and holding power over others. Systemic racism is a myth that makes SJWs think that they will always have a place in society even though they won't. Like BLM, SJWs will be tossed aside once their time is done, the only problem is that those poor bastards will be marched into the showers after they push everyone else in and they are the only people left besides those in charge. They won't mind either, according to the book White Fragility by Robin DiAngelo, if you are white, you are racist and that cannot be changed. A good SJW should be willing to walk into a shower or even an oven if it is the final proof needed to show they are not racist. Like any good little cult member, the Kool-Aid will be passed around and they will drink every drop.

"SARS-CoV-2 causes COVID-19." Page 136.

Maybe I am a complete idiot or this is just a poorly written statement. As a man who took microbiology, worked in the healthcare field, and has several friends who work in medicine I have no idea what the hell this statement is. I understand that HIV turns into AIDS. I know that the flu and other illnesses can turn into pneumonia. My understanding of Covid-19 is that it is SARS-CoV-2. Covid-19 is the strain of the corona virus that causes severe acute respiratory syndrome. This statement from the book leads me to ask, are they testing people for Covid-19 or SARS-CoV-2? And why is it that certain lab techs can't get a sample of Covid-19 to compare samples to? I'm sure that some people out there will have a simple explanation for this and I will look like a complete fool but this short statement in the middle of

the book sounds like non-sense.

How to stop the Great Reset

It is a tall order to say that the common man can stop something as well organized as the Great Reset. We have the book by Klaus Schwab, Agenda 2030 and 2050 by the United Nations, and a push to keep Covid-19 relevant even though the survival rate is 99.9%. It would appear that we have a decade, maybe less with the 2030 date ticking away and in reality, I would say we have 3-5 years to stop this. Do you want to live a life where you own nothing, have no privacy, have every choice monitored, and they say you will be happy? Why do I think we have 3-5 years?

The initial plan ends with 2030. That only happens if the first steps are taken and they are able to continue on their path of control. Keep in mind, Covid-19 is an important aspect of this plan, it is the excuse they grasp on to so that they can suppress individual rights and start grinding away at documents like the constitution. We are seeing some progress against the Great Reset. Government mandated Covid passports were found to be unconstitutional so instead we are seeing a push for businesses to violate your medical privacy by requiring proof you were vaccinated. I think that some will try this and maybe there will be a requirement on your actual passport for travel, but keep in mind infected people were allowed to travel for the last year. Vaccines are mandated to travel to some countries already, what we could see is a state-by-state mandate for proof of vaccination still violating HIPPA laws and I would like to think they would be found a violation of constitutional law. The only downside is the cost in lawsuits to overturn laws that were already a violation of the laws we have now.

As a write this Texas, Georgia, Florida, Indiana, Montana, and several others that are no longer locked down or were never locked down like North Dakota, Utah, and Nebraska are completely open for business. The smaller governments become the easier it is to bypass the great reset. Today, President Biden signed executive orders for gun laws that are unconstitutional. In response, states signed laws to not follow federal gun laws. That doesn't mean that the ATF can't enforce those laws but it does create a barrier to make it easy to enforce. Then we have these horrible promises to make gasoline fueled vehicles banned from various countries by 2030. The UK signed a law to make this happen along with a few others, and the US is wanting to do the same thing. What they don't realize is that this would also include farm equipment, transportation of goods, and airliners. Before the year 1900 it was uncommon for most people on the planet to travel further that 5 miles from their home. This is what they want to go back to. By eliminating fossil fuels, we will also lose fertilizers, pesticides, plastic to wrap and ship produce, trucks with refrigeration, tractors to plant, harvest, plow, bale, weed, etc. It would appear that those in power have no desire to feed the public, the common man, over the next decade. As for the push towards renewable energy, the latest calamity in Texas and Germany during a late winter storm showed the rest of the world green energy isn't where it needs to be if it's going to work to replace the grid system we have now.

There was a phrase that became famous during the 1980s, perhaps it has been long forgotten. "Just say no," was something Nancy Reagan said about doing drugs. If you believe in the great reset or any of the woke SJW bullshit that is coming out of government or Hollywood, you deserve to be looked upon as a drug addict who is not thinking rationally. Granted, just say no, didn't do much to curb the drug problem in the country and DARE ended up teaching kids how to do drugs that they weren't familiar with. The one drug we should be avoiding at this point is socialist/ communist ideology that is being pumped out by our news media and the woke left who desire to control everyone while promising everything.

There are two stories being told by the media these days, Covid-19 cases are spiking and cases are dropping. In my state of Michigan, we are allegedly seeing a spike in cases that is causing the Governor to start voluntary lockdowns while her assistant takes a trip to Florida for vacation followed by herself going to Florida. Meanwhile in Florida, Texas, and other states, case numbers are dropping and the states are completely open for business. It would appear that the states which continue lockdowns, for some reason, see a spike in cases while states with no restrictions see low numbers of cases. It isn't difficult to see that either cases spike from lockdowns, or the states engaging in lockdowns might be taking liberties with the numbers they are reporting. As we know about government and other businesses, if your paycheck depends on the continuation of a problem, it is best not to solve that problem.

It is important for people to engage in civil disobedience when it comes to the Great Reset, Covid-19, and BLM. All of these agendas go hand in hand and work together for the same goal. There is a two-tier system at work here. The first is to pass policies through government, and when they can't use government, corporations will be used to make social changes. We are already seeing this with Facebook and Twitter, two social media apps I don't use. So, what can we do?

Get off of social media. At least the festering cesspools that are Facebook and Twitter. Don't let these corporations collect your information and create profiles on you. Be careful where you spend your money. Buy local and small when you can. For every dollar these large corporations don't collect it is less power they have over us. Support independent media and don't watch major media outlets. They don't give you news anyway. Stay in the control group. Get the vaccine if that is what you decide to do, I however will sit back and watch what happens to those who do take it. If they want to use the public for an experiment, I will volunteer to be part of the control group to see what the side effects are. Don't follow stupid laws that are not based on science. 6 feet, 3 feet, mask, no mask, double mask, none of these guidelines made sense since day one. Airborne diseases are difficult to contract and keeping people indoors makes it easier to contract an airborne illness. If you want the public to contract a disease, continue the lockdown. Start local trade. Find people to trade goods with. With food shortages, freighters getting stuck in canals, and new regulations preventing farmers from doing their jobs we will need to find local sources of necessary goods. There is more and I'm sure I will think of other things to add as soon as I post this. The important thing is to get started on the

resistance. Think for yourself. Question authority.

Manufactured by Amazon.ca
Bolton, ON

26305414R00067